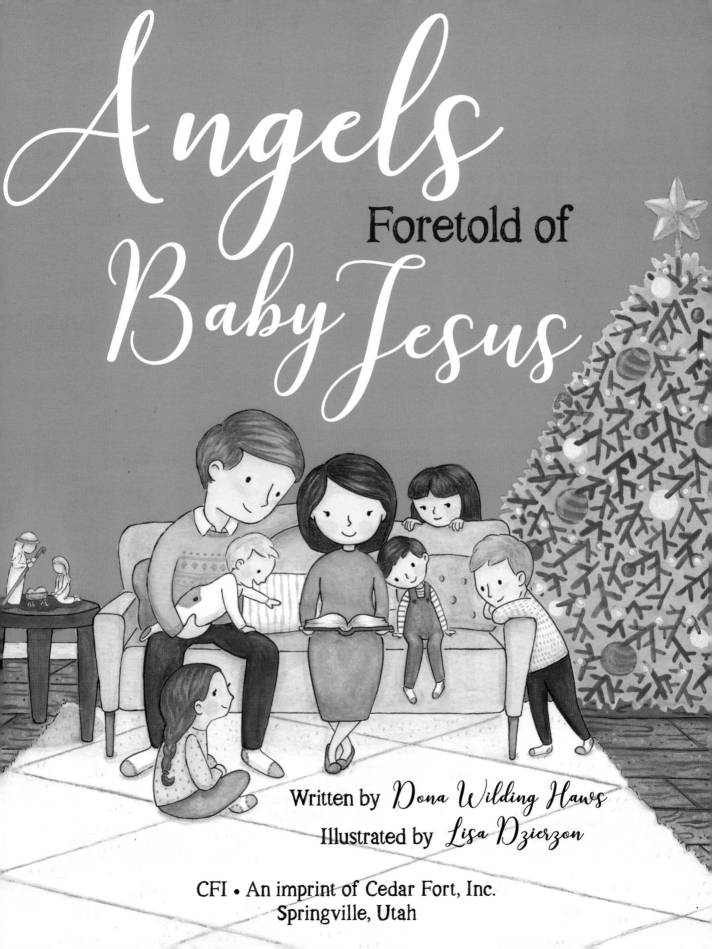

Angels Foretold of Baby Jesus

Written by *Dona Wilding Haws*

Illustrated by *Lisa Dzierzon*

CFI • An imprint of Cedar Fort, Inc.
Springville, Utah

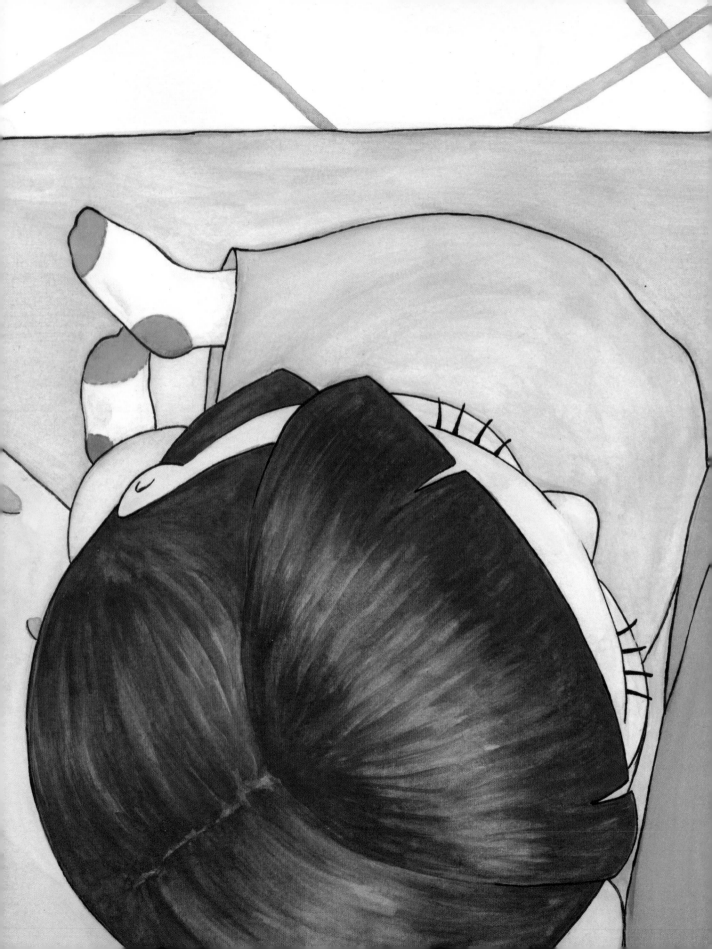

Long, long ago,

ISAIAH saw the Lord sitting on His throne with angels all around. Isaiah prophesied that the Lord would come to earth. He would be called Wonderful, Counselor, the Prince of Peace.

Long, long ago,

LEHI had a heavenly dream. He learned that the Messiah would be the Savior of the world. He would be baptized.

He would give up His life, and three days later,
He would rise from the dead to live forever.

1 Nephi
11:14–21
2 Nephi
25:19–23

Long, long ago,

God sent an angel to **NEPHI**. "Look!" said the angel.
"Behold the Lamb of God."

NEPHI looked and saw the beautiful
MARY holding her precious baby.
He would be named **JESUS CHRIST**.

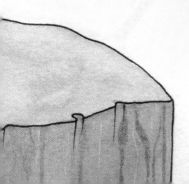

Long, long ago,

KING BENJAMIN saw an angel, who spoke to him, saying, "hear the words which I shall tell thee; for behold, I am come to declare unto you the glad tidings of great joy."

KING BENJAMIN learned that Jesus would
"go forth amongst men, working mighty miracles."

Long, long ago,

just five years before Jesus came, God sent an angel to **SAMUEL**, a Lamanite.

SAMUEL prophesied that before the Savior's birth, "There shall be great lights in heaven . . .

and behold, there shall a new star arise."

Long, long ago,

just before Jesus came, God sent **ANGEL GABRIEL** to **ZACHARIAS**, an old priest. Gabriel told Zacharias, "Thy wife **ELIZABETH** shall bear thee a son, and thou shalt call his name **JOHN**."

When baby John grew up, people called him **JOHN THE BAPTIST,** and he baptized Jesus.

Long, long ago,

the **ANGEL GABRIEL** told **MARY**, "Fear not, Mary, for thou hast found favour with God … thou shalt … bring forth a son."

Long, long ago,

the same **ANGEL GABRIEL** told **JOSEPH** that Mary would have a Son and to **"Call his name JESUS"**

As **ISAIAH** saw . . .

Isaiah
6:1–2, 9:6

And as **LEHI** saw . . .

And as the angel told
KING BENJAMIN . . .

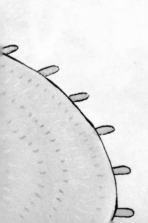

Mosiah
3:2-8

And as the angel told
SAMUEL, the Lamanite . . .

ZARAHEMLA

THIS WAY

2 MILES

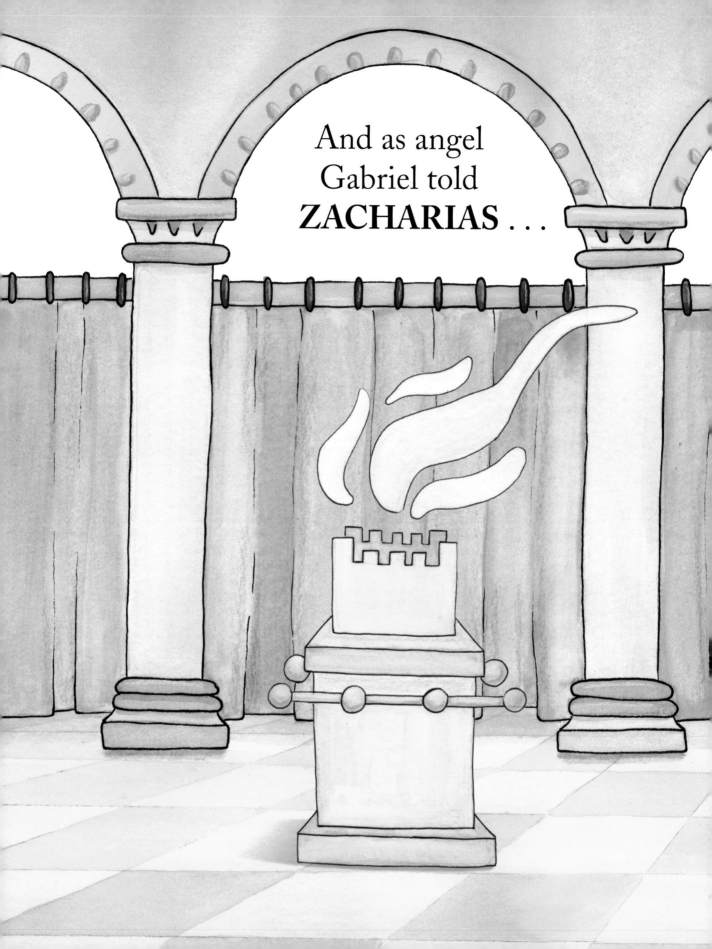

And as angel
Gabriel told
ZACHARIAS . . .

And as angel Gabriel told **MARY** . . .

And as the angel told **JOSEPH** . . .

THE SAVIOR
OF THE WORLD
WAS BORN!

To Jacob, Emmaline, Samuel, Abigail,
Zoe, Zachary, and all God's children.
–Dona

To my children, Finnley and Alvin, who inspire me.
And to my husband, Christoph, thank you for your
endless encouragement, support, and love.
–Lisa

Text © 2017 Dona Haws
Illustrations © 2017 Lisa Dzierzon
All rights reserved.

This is not an official publication of The Church of Jesus Christ of Latter-day Saints. The
opinions and views expressed herein belong solely to the author and do not necessarily
represent the opinions or views of Cedar Fort, Inc. Permission for the use of sources,
graphics, and photos is also solely the responsibility of the author.

ISBN 13: 978-1-4621-1987-5

Published by CFI, an imprint of Cedar Fort, Inc.
2373 W. 700 S., Springville, UT 84663
Distributed by Cedar Fort, Inc., www.cedarfort.com

Cover design and typesetting by Shawnda T. Craig & Kinsey Beckett
Cover design © 2017 Cedar Fort, Inc.
Edited by Kaitlin Barwick

Printed in the United States of America

10 9 8 7 6 5 4 3 2

Printed on acid-free paper